SUPPER

— WITH —

Mrs BEETON

DELICIOUS SPREADS

SUPPER

— WITH —

Mrs BEETON

DELICIOUS SPREADS

WARD LOCK

First published 1991 by Ward Lock
Villiers House, 41/47 Strand, London WC2N 5JE, England

A Cassell imprint

British Library Cataloguing in Publication Data
Supper with Mrs Beeton.
1. Food, History
642.1

ISBN 0-7063-7037-6

Designed by Cherry Randell
Illustrations by Mike Shoebridge

Typeset in Goudy Old Style by Litho Link Ltd, Welshpool, Powys, Wales

Printed and bound in Gt. Britain by Bath Colourbooks Ltd

◈◈◈◈◈◈◈◈◈◈◈◈◈◈◈

1 cup breadcrumbs = 50 g/2 oz
1 cup butter = 225 g/8 oz
1 cup caster (superfine) sugar = 200 g/7 oz
1 cup cheese (grated) = 100 g/4 oz
1 cup chicken (chopped) = 150 g/5 oz
1 cup flour = 100 g/4 oz
1 cup mushrooms (chopped) = 75 g/3 oz
1 cup peas (cooked) = 150 g/5oz

◈◈◈◈◈◈◈◈◈◈◈◈◈◈◈

CONTENTS

$\mathscr{I}$NTRODUCTION

Victorian families usually took the first meal of the day at about eight o'clock in the morning so that the gentlemen of the household had time for a hearty breakfast before going off to their places of work.

Lunch was a light meal of soup and a sandwich or similar dishes to breakfast. If a lady entertained her friends to luncheon, the family cook would prepare dainty and

elegant galantines (dishes of layered, pressed meats) or cold joints of beef or venison. The food had to be reasonably easy to manage since ladies ate this meal still wearing their hats and jackets. Children meanwhile ate their lunch of meat and two vegetables, followed by a pudding with custard, with their nanny up in the day nursery. If their mother was alone she often shared their meal.

The next meal of the day was afternoon tea, when society ladies called on each other, gossiped and partook of cups of tea, champagne cup or sherry, and dainty sandwiches, cakes and fancy biscuits. Then came dinner at eight or half-past. A typical meal consisted of six or seven courses of elaborate dishes, although family dinners were a little more modest and included dishes made from left-over meats and vegetables. The youngest children had a nursery tea at about 4 o'clock, with a hot drink and bread and butter or biscuits before going to bed.

Earlier in the century dinner had been served at six or seven o'clock and a late supper was therefore often taken before bedtime. However, in 1861, Mrs Beeton wrote, 'Hot suppers are now very little in request, as people now generally dine at an hour which precludes the possibility of requiring supper.'

Families sometimes shared a supper of cold meats, pickles, fruit, cheese and biscuits, but the most fashionable supper in the second half of the nineteenth century was the Supper Dance, Ball or Reception. At these, a buffet table, draped with garlands of flowers, was laid out with a vast selection of cold fish and meat dishes, patties and pies, galantines and salads, jellies, custards, meringues and charlottes with decorative epergnes of fresh fruit, sweetmeats and fancy pastries. The dishes were ornately garnished with aspic jellies, vegetables, flowers and spun sugar. Such splendid displays were quite different from the rather modest fare that we today would enjoy as an informal evening meal or as a refreshment after a visit to the theatre.

$\mathscr{S}$OUPS

Soups are much simpler to make today than in Mrs Beeton's time. Blenders and food processors enable the modern cook to produce delicious soups that are ideal for supper quickly and easily.

FRENCH ONION SOUP

50 g/2 oz fat bacon, chopped
6 onions, thinly sliced
15 g/½ oz plain flour
salt and pepper
2.5 ml/½ tsp French mustard
900 ml/1½ pints stock
150 ml/¼ pint white wine or cider
6 small slices of bread
butter
*50 g/2 oz Gruyère **or** Parmesan cheese, grated*

Heat the bacon gently in a deep saucepan until the fat runs freely. Fry the onions slowly in the bacon fat until golden. Add the flour, salt and pepper to taste and continue frying for a few minutes. Stir in the mustard, stock and wine or cider.

Simmer until the onions are quite soft.

Toast the bread. Butter the toast and spread the slices with the grated cheese. Pour the soup into individual flameproof soup-bowls, float a round of toast on each and brown it under the grill.

SERVES 6

MULLIGATAWNY SOUP

*450 g/1 lb lean mutton **or** rabbit **or**
stewing veal **or** shin of beef **or** ox tail
25 g/1 oz butter **or** margarine
1 onion, finely chopped
15 g/½ oz curry powder
1 small cooking apple, finely chopped
25 g/1 oz plain flour
1.1 litres/2 pints bone stock **or** water
salt
1 carrot
½ small parsnip
a bunch of herbs
lemon juice
1.25 ml/¼ tsp black treacle (optional)
50 g/2 oz long-grain rice, cooked*

Cut the meat in small pieces. Heat
the butter or margarine in a deep
pan and quickly fry the onion, then
the curry powder. Add the apple
and cook it gently for a few
minutes, then stir in the flour. Add
the stock or water, meat and a little
salt, and bring slowly to simmering
point, stirring all the time.

Add the other vegetables, the
herbs tied in muslin and a few drops
of lemon juice. Simmer until the
meat is very tender. This will take
between 2 hours for rabbit and 4
hours for shin of beef. Taste the
soup and add more lemon juice or
add black treacle to obtain a flavour
that is neither predominantly sweet
nor acid. Strain the soup, cut some
of the meat in neat cubes and
reheat them in the soup. Hand the
boiled rice separately.

Note The amount of curry powder
may be varied to taste; the quantity
given is for a mild-flavoured soup.

SERVES 4 TO 6

FISH CHOWDER

*900 g/2 lb filleted fish, cod **or** haddock,*
the head, bones and skin of the fish
150 ml/¼ pint water
salt and pepper
lemon rind
a bunch of herbs
a blade of mace
100 g/4 oz salt pork
2 onions, thinly sliced
450 g/1 lb potatoes, diced
25 g/1 oz plain flour
600 ml/1 pint milk
25 g/1 oz butter

Skin the filleted fish. Make a fish stock with the water, bones, head and skin of the fish, salt, lemon rind, herbs and mace, simmering gently for 30 minutes.

Cut the fillets into 5 cm/2 inch strips. Cut the pork in tiny cubes and heat it gently in a deep pan until the fat flows freely. In the pork fat cook the onion without browning for 10 minutes, then add the potatoes and shake them well in the fat for a few minutes. Sprinkle in the flour. Gradually add the hot, strained stock, then put in the pieces of fish and season the soup. Cook very gently for 30 minutes.

Heat the milk and butter together and add to the soup when the fish and potatoes are soft. Do not reboil. Serve at once.

SERVES 4 TO 6

ON THE SIDE

As a change from the usual bread and rolls try the following as accompaniments to soup:

✶ Croûtons – cut bread into little stars or hearts with small pastry cutters and fry in hot oil or butter until crisp. Spoon into the soup just before serving or put in a pretty bowl and hand round.

✶ Pitta fingers – split rounds of pitta bread along one edge and spread the insides with herb or garlic butter. Close up, warm in the oven, cut into neat fingers and serve hot.

✶ Melba toast – lightly toast both sides of slices of bread with the crusts left on, then cut off the crusts, split each slice through the middle and toast the other sides until pale golden (be careful, they burn easily).

✶ Muffins – toast whole white or brown muffins, then split and spread with cream cheese mixed with chopped fresh chives, or with garlic butter. Put back together, cut in half neatly and serve hot.

MINESTRONE

100 g/4 oz haricot beans
1.75 litres/3 pints water
30 ml/2 tbsp olive oil
2 onions, sliced
1–2 garlic cloves, crushed
25 g/1 oz lean bacon scraps, chopped
a bunch of herbs
2 large tomatoes, roughly chopped
150 ml/¼ pint red wine
2 carrots, diced
1 small turnip, diced
2 celery sticks, diced
2 small potatoes, diced
½ small cabbage, shredded
50 g/2 oz macaroni
salt and pepper
grated cheese

Soak the beans overnight in cold water. Drain, put in a saucepan with 300 ml/½ pint of the water and bring to the boil. Boil rapidly for 10 minutes. Set aside.

Heat the oil in a deep pan and fry the onions very gently for 10 minutes. Add the garlic, bacon, herbs, tomatoes and wine. Reduce this mixture by rapid boiling for 5 minutes. Add the haricot beans and all the water and simmer for 2 hours. Add the carrot, turnip and celery to the soup; simmer for a further 30 minutes. Then add the potatoes, and simmer for another 30 minutes. Add the shredded cabbage and the macaroni and simmer for a final 10–15 minutes. Add salt and pepper to taste. Stir a little grated cheese into the soup and serve some more separately.

SERVES 6

SOUR CHERRY SOUP

450 g/1 lb Morello **or** *other acid*
variety of cherry
a pinch of ground cinnamon
600 ml/1 pint water
to each 600 ml/1 pint sieved soup:
15 g/½ oz cornflour, arrowroot **or**
minute tapioca
75–100 g/3–4 oz caster sugar
150 ml/¼ pint white **or** *red wine*
(optional)
a little lemon rind
whipped cream (optional)

Halve the cherries and crack some of the stones. Put the cherries, stones, cinnamon and water into a saucepan and simmer until the cherries are soft. Rub the fruit through a hair or nylon sieve.

Blend the cornflour with a little wine or water and stir it into the soup. Reboil and stir the soup until it thickens. Sweeten, add the wine (if used) and grated lemon rind.

The soup may be served hot or iced. Whipped cream (served separately) makes a delicious accompaniment.

SERVES 4

THE STOCK POT

Mrs Beeton wrote in 1861, 'We are glad to note that soups of vegetables, fish, meat and game are now very frequently found in the homes of the English Middle Classes, as well as in the mansions of the wealthier and more aristocratic.' A good stock, in her opinion, was the basis for all soups, and large kitchens always had two stock pots: one for making pale soups and one for darker varieties.

Both stocks were made from meat bones, oddments of meat, vegetables and herbs.

The pot was simmered all day, then the stock was strained and skimmed to remove any fat. Thin consommés were clarified with egg shells and egg whites. Thick soups were puréed by working the mixture through a 'tamis' – a thick piece of cloth.

FISH

Fresh fish is an excellent choice for a light meal. It is low in fat, high in protein, and speedily cooked. It is filling and satisfying without being too rich.

SALMON MOUSSE

600 ml/1 pint clear fish stock
25 g/1 oz gelatine
salt and pepper
2 egg whites
450 g/1 lb cooked salmon

Put 60 ml/4 tbsp of the stock in a small bowl and sprinkle the gelatine on top. Stand the bowl over a saucepan of hot water and stir the gelatine until it has dissolved completely. Add salt and pepper to taste.

Cook the egg whites in a dariole mould or small cup until firm; when cold cut into thin slices and cut out in fancy shapes.

Drain the oil from the salmon and remove all skin and bones.

Cover the bottom of a mould with the jellied stock, leave to set, and then garnish with egg white shapes. Set the garnish with a little jelly, allow to set. Add a layer of salmon, cover with jelly and put aside until set. Repeat until the mould is full. Keep in the refrigerator or in a cool place until wanted, then turn out and serve.

SERVES 6 TO 8

THE IMPORTANCE
OF FISH

'In dressing fish of any kind, the first point to be attended to, is to see that it is perfectly clean. It is a common error to wash it too much, as by doing so the flavour is diminished . . . Fish should be put into cold water and set on the fire to do very gently, or the outside will break before the inner part is done . . . If fish is to be fried or broiled it must be dried in a nice soft cloth after it is well cleaned and washed. If for frying, brush it over with egg, and sprinkle it with some fine crumbs of bread . . . When fish is broiled, it must be seasoned, floured, and laid on a very clean gridiron, which, when hot, should be rubbed with a bit of suet, to prevent the fish from sticking. It must be broiled over a very clear fire, that it may not taste smoky; and not too near, that it may not be scorched . . . Nothing can be of greater consequence to a cook than to have the fish good; as, if this important course in a dinner does not give satisfaction, it is rarely that the repast goes off well.'

Mrs Beeton
Book of Household Management, 1861

CURRIED PRAWNS

24 whole cooked prawns
40 g/1½ oz butter
1 small onion, finely
chopped
10–15 ml/2–3 tsp curry powder
10 ml/2 tsp plain flour
300 ml/½ pint stock
1 cooking apple, coarsely chopped
15 ml/1 tbsp grated coconut
salt and pepper
15 ml/1 tbsp lemon juice

Shell the prawns and put aside. Melt the butter in a saucepan and fry the onion without browning. Add the curry powder and flour and fry gently for at least 20 minutes. Then add the stock, apple, coconut and a little salt. Simmer for 30 minutes, then strain and return to the pan. Add the lemon juice and salt and pepper to taste. Put in the prawns and when thoroughly hot, serve with boiled rice.

SERVES 4

HADDOCK CROUSTADES

1 small dried haddock (smoked)
25 g/1 oz butter
2 eggs
30 ml/2 tbsp milk
a good pinch of pepper
a grating of nutmeg
croustades of bread
cayenne

Cook the haddock in boiling water until just tender. Flake all the fish away from the bones. Melt the butter in a saucepan, and when hot add the eggs, beaten with the milk, and pepper, flaked haddock and nutmeg. Cook very gently until lightly set.

Fill the mixture into croustades of bread and garnish with cayenne.

SERVES 4

CROUSTADES OF BREAD

Stamp out 5 cm/1 inch circles or ovals from 2 cm/¾ inch thick slices of bread. With a smaller cutter make an inner circle or oval about 5 mm/¼ inch from the outer edge. Fry the shapes in hot fat until lightly browned. Drain, then with the point of a small knife lift out the inner ring and remove any moist crumb.

grill at the same time, for garnish.

Meanwhile prepare the gooseberries, stew in a very little water, or in their own juice if bottled or canned. Sweeten slightly if necessary, rub through a sieve and return the purée to the saucepan. Stir in the grated nutmeg and reheat (reduce by rapid boiling if necessary.)

Serve the fillets on a hot dish, garnished with the tomatoes and serve the sauce separately.

SERVES 4

GRILLED MACKEREL WITH GOOSEBERRY SAUCE

2 large mackerel
15 ml/1 tbsp seasoned plain flour
25 g/1 oz margarine
tomatoes
225 g/8 oz gooseberries **or** *a small*
bottle **or** *can of gooseberries*
1.25 ml/¼ tsp grated nutmeg

Trim, clean and fillet the mackerel. Dip each fillet in seasoned flour. Melt the margarine in the bottom of the grill pan, add the fillets, brush them with the melted fat and grill for 8–10 minutes, turning once. Cut the tomatoes in half and

HALIBUT BRISTOL

butter for greasing
450 g/1 lb halibut (centre cut)
salt and pepper
150 ml/¼ pint milk and water
15 g/½ oz butter **or** *margarine*
15 g/½ oz plain flour
40 g/1½ oz grated cheese
12 mussels (fresh-cooked)

Set the oven at 190°C/375°F/gas 5.

Put the halibut in a greased ovenproof dish, sprinkle with a little salt and pepper and add the liquid. Cover with greased paper and cook for 20 minutes.

Remove from the oven, strain off the liquid and remove the centre bone from the fish. Set the oven at 230°C/450°F/gas 8. Use the fish liquid to make a creamy sauce with the fat and flour, add 25 g/1 oz of the cheese and salt and pepper if necessary. Arrange the mussels round the halibut, cover all with the sauce and sprinkle over the remaining cheese. Return the dish to the oven for a further 10 minutes to brown.

SERVES 4

$\mathcal{L}$IGHT SAVOURIES

In Victorian days, savouries formed the final course of a dinner before the dessert. Today, such dishes are just enough for a light supper when something tasty, but not rich and heavy, is required.

GOLDEN BUCK

100 g/4 oz Cheshire **or** *Cheddar cheese, finely grated*
15 g/½ oz butter
45 ml/3 tbsp ale
2.5 ml/½ tsp Worcestershire sauce
2.5 ml/½ tsp lemon juice **or** *vinegar*
2 eggs, beaten
a pinch of celery salt
a pinch of cayenne
2 large slices buttered toast
chopped parsley

Put the cheese into a saucepan with the butter and ale and stir vigorously until creamy. Then add the Worcestershire sauce, lemon juice or vinegar and the eggs. Season to taste with celery salt and cayenne, and continue stirring briskly until the mixture thickens.

Trim the toast, and cover with the cheese mixture. Garnish with parsley. Serve as hot as possible.

SERVES 2 TO 4

TASTY EXTRAS

As a change from rolls or toast, try the following:

**** Pastry shapes – roll out some puff pastry and sprinkle liberally with grated cheese and/or sesame, poppy or onion seeds/or herbs. Fold into three, roll and fold twice more, then cut into fingers, rounds or shapes. Put on a baking sheet, brush with beaten egg and bake in a hot oven until crisp and golden.

**** Herb or garlic bread – made with a crusty loaf or French stick.

**** Crumpets – toasted until crisp and golden and spread with garlic or herb butter.

**** Potato farls – split through the middle, buttered and spread with cream cheese, put back together and cut into neat fingers.

EGGS MORNAY

butter for greasing
4 hard-boiled eggs
25 g/1 oz butter
grated nutmeg
40 g/1½ oz cheese, grated
150 ml/¼ pint white sauce
salt and pepper

Cut the eggs into thick slices and place them on a well-buttered flameproof dish. Sprinkle them lightly with nutmeg and more liberally with salt and pepper. Add 25 g/1 oz of the cheese to the sauce and pour it over the eggs. Sprinkle thickly with the remaining cheese, and add a few tiny pieces of butter. Brown the surface under the grill and serve.

SERVES 4

CHEESE RAMEKINS

15 ml/1 tbsp breadcrumbs
boiling milk
25 g/1 oz Parmesan cheese, grated
25 g/1 oz Cheshire cheese, grated
25 g/1 oz butter
1 egg, separated
salt and pepper
mace

Set the oven at 220°C/425°F/gas 7. Put the breadcrumbs in a bowl and barely cover with boiling milk. Leave to stand for 10 minutes. Stir well. Add the cheeses, butter, egg yolk and salt and pepper to taste. Beat until the mixture is quite smooth. Whisk the egg white to a stiff froth and fold it into the mixture. Pour into well-greased ramekin dishes and bake in the oven until set – about 8–10 minutes.

SERVES 4 TO 6

MUSHROOM SOUFFLE

25 g/1 oz butter **or** *margarine*
25 g/1 oz plain flour
150 ml/¼ pint milk
100 g/4 oz mushrooms, very finely chopped
3 eggs, separated
salt and pepper
1 egg white

Set the oven at 190°C/375°F/gas 5.

Melt the butter or margarine in a saucepan, stir in the flour and cook for several minutes, stirring well. Gradually add the milk, bring to the boil and cook until thickened. Add the mushrooms and egg yolks with salt and pepper to taste. Lastly fold in all the stiffly beaten egg whites. Fill into a well greased soufflé dish, and bake for about 30 minutes.

Serve at once.

SERVES 4

23

CHICKEN CROQUETTES

25 g/1 oz butter
25 g/1 oz plain flour
150 ml/¼ pint stock
225 g/8 oz cold chicken, boned and finely chopped
50 g/2 oz cooked ham, finely chopped
6 button mushrooms, chopped
15 ml/1 tbsp single cream
5 ml/1 tsp lemon juice
salt and pepper
beaten egg
fresh breadcrumbs
fat for frying

Melt the butter in a saucepan, stir in the flour, and add the stock slowly. Cook for 3–5 minutes. Add all the other ingredients, and turn on to a plate to cool.

Form the mixture into cork-shapes, coat with egg and breadcrumbs, and fry until golden brown in hot deep fat. Drain and serve on a doily-covered dish.

SERVES 6

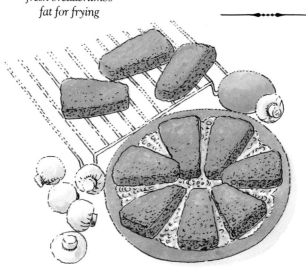

Sprinkle this mixture over the livers. Wrap the rashers of bacon round the livers, and fasten them in position with skewers. Cook under the grill. Remove the skewers, put 2 bacon rolls on each croûte of bread, and serve as hot as possible.

SERVES 4

DEVILLED CHICKENS' LIVERS

4 chickens' livers
1 shallot or small onion, finely chopped
2.5 ml/½ tsp chopped parsley
a pinch of cayenne
a pinch of salt
8 small rashers of bacon
4 croûtes of fried bread

Wash and dry the livers, cut them in halves. Mix the shallot or onion with the parsley, cayenne and salt.

SUMMER SUPPER

sour cherry soup

duck salad with French dressing

raspberry and yogurt delight
or
fruit and cheese

CALF'S LIVER AND BACON

450 g/1 lb calf's liver, cut in 5 mm/
¼ inch thick slices
salt and pepper
plain flour
225 g/8 oz bacon, cut in thin rashers
25 g/1 oz butter

Dip the pieces of liver in some seasoned flour. Heat a frying pan, put in the bacon, and fry slowly. Keep hot until wanted. Fry the liver in the bacon fat until nicely browned on both sides, then remove to a hot dish.

Discard the bacon fat, and add the butter. Sprinkle in about 15 ml/ 1 tbsp flour, stir and fry until brown. Add about 300 ml/½ pint warm water, stir until it boils, and add salt and pepper to taste. Arrange the pieces of liver in a close circle, strain the gravy over, place the bacon rashers on the top, and serve.

SERVES 4 TO 6

WINTER SUPPER

mulligatawny soup
served with hot muffins

golden buck
with chutneys and pickles

Bakewell pudding
with yogurt or cream

SAUTEED KIDNEYS

6 sheep's kidneys
25 g/1 oz butter
2 shallots, finely chopped
150 ml/¼ pint brown sauce
15 ml/1 tbsp sherry (optional)
salt and pepper
*croûtes of fried **or** toasted bread*
watercress

Skin the kidneys and remove the cores. Soak for 5 minutes in cold water. Dry and cut into 5 mm/ ¼ inch slices.

Melt the butter in a sauté pan and fry the shallots slightly. Then add the sliced kidney and shake and toss over the heat for about 5 minutes. Drain off the surplus fat and add the brown sauce, sherry (if used) and salt and pepper. Stir over a gentle heat until thoroughly hot, but take care not to let the mixture boil.

Serve as hot as possible on toast or fried bread, garnished with watercress.

SERVES 6

$\mathcal{P}$IES

*Raised pies were a popular feature of Victorian suppers,
the most common variety being pigeon pie. Today's pies
are less elaborate and ornate than their predecessors, but
they still make a tasty 'meal-in-one'.*

VEGETABLE PIE

*2 onions
2 carrots
2 celery sticks
a few mushrooms
10 ml/2 tsp plain flour
salt and pepper
a few green peas
25 g/1 oz sago **or** tapioca
50 g/2 oz butter
1 quantity short crust pastry (page 46)
using wholemeal flour*

Set the oven at 190°C/375°F/gas 5.

Cut the onions, carrots, celery
and mushrooms into small pieces.
Dip them in seasoned flour and put
into a saucepan with the peas, sago
or tapioca and a very little water.
Stew until they are three-quarters
cooked, then put them in a pie dish

and place the butter in small dabs
on top. Cover with the pastry and
bake for about 30 minutes, until
the crust is cooked.

Note The pie may be made of any
vegetables that are in season.

SERVES 4

BIRDS IN THEIR COFFINS

Pies date back to the eleventh or twelfth century and were usually made with a raised crust in the shape of a loaf. Birds of all varieties were popular fillings, and the plumage was used to decorate the 'coffins', so that guests at a feast would know what was inside the crust.

In Victorian days, raised pies were often baked in a decorative mould which imprinted a very ornate design on the pastry case. The tops were usually decorated with leaves and other shapes cut from the pastry trimmings, but three or four pigeon's feet were always stuck upside down in the top of pigeon pie.

HAM AND EGG PIE

100 g/4 oz mushrooms
60 ml/4 tbsp milk
salt and pepper
175–225 g/6–8 oz cooked ham
75 g/3 oz cooked peas
2 hard-boiled eggs
50 ml/1 tsp prepared mustard

FLAKY PASTRY
225 g/8 oz plain flour
a pinch of salt
*275 g/10 oz butter (**or** half butter,*
half lard)
2.5 ml/½ tsp lemon juice
*beaten egg **or** milk*

To make the pastry, sift the flour and salt into a bowl. Divide the fat into four equal portions and lightly rub a quarter of it into the flour. Mix to a soft dough with cold water and lemon juice. Roll out into an oblong and place a quarter of the butter in small pieces on the top third of the pastry. Dredge lightly with flour, fold up the bottom third of the pastry on to the fat and fold down the top third. Press the edges together lightly with a rolling pin and half-turn the pastry. Roll out as before. Repeat the process with the remaining portions of butter. If possible, allow the pastry to relax in a cool place between rollings.

Set the oven at 230°C/450°F/gas 8. Simmer the mushrooms for 10 minutes in the milk with salt and pepper to taste. Mix the ham with the remaining ingredients. Divide the pastry into two unequal portions. Roll out the larger piece and cover an ovenproof dish or plate. Trim the edges and put in the prepared filling. Use the remaining pastry to cover the pie. Decorate as wished and glaze the top with beaten egg or milk. Bake until set, then reduce the oven temperature to 160°C/325°F/gas 3, cooking for about 45 minutes in all.

SERVES 4

CHEESE AND ONION TART

3 small onions, sliced
1 quantity short crust pastry (page 42)
salt and pepper
15 g/½ oz plain flour
100 g/4 oz cheese, grated
30 ml/2 tbsp milk

Set the oven at 220°C/425°F/gas 7.

Parboil the onions whilst making the pastry. Line a 20 cm/8 inch ovenproof plate with the pastry. Mix the salt and pepper with the flour. Dip the onion slices in the seasoned flour, spread them over the bottom of the lined plate. Sprinkle the cheese over the onion, and add the milk. Brush over the pastry edge with milk and bake for about 30 minutes, until the onions are tender.

SERVES 6 TO 8

$\mathscr{S}$ALADS

*With such a variety of vegetables and fruit now available,
it is simple to create colourful salads that make perfect
supper dishes. Try different dressings to complement the
mixtures and bring out the flavours.*

DUCK SALAD

*½ a cold duck
1 small celery heart
salt and pepper
45 ml/3 tbsp French dressing
2 slices unpeeled orange
1 cabbage lettuce
a small bunch of watercress
mayonnaise
5 ml/1 tsp chopped parsley
5 ml/1 tsp chopped olives*

Cut the duck into 2.5 cm/1 inch
dice, and the celery into fine strips.
Mix in a bowl with salt and pepper
to taste and 30 ml/2 tbsp of the
French dressing, and leave to stand.

Cut the orange slices into
quarters or eighths. Line the salad
bowl with lettuce leaves and sprigs
of watercress. Garnish with the
orange sections and baste with the
remaining French dressing. Place
the duck mixture in the centre and
cover with a thin layer of
mayonnaise. Sprinkle with parsley
and olives.

SERVES 6

ITALIAN SALAD

225 g/8 oz cold roast veal, diced
225 g/8 oz cooked potatoes, diced
100 g/4 oz beetroot, diced
100 g/4 oz gherkins, sliced
15 ml/1 tbsp capers
salt and pepper
*mayonnaise **or** French dressing*
12 stoned olives
crisp lettuce leaves
12 slices salami sausage
1 lemon, sliced

SUPPER ON A TRAY

A tray should be arranged as
carefully as a table, with as much
thought being given to colour and
style, mood and occasion. Cover
the tray with a cloth to suit the
colour scheme and arrange a
napkin and cutlery to one side.
Place a small salt and pepper set in
one corner and a glass in another.

Do not clutter the tray with
dishes of butter or extra pickles or
chutneys. Instead, arrange all the
food beautifully on one plate,
buttering the roll or bread
beforehand. Make room for a single
flower or a tiny vase with a small
posy of fresh flowers.

Mix the veal, potatoes, beetroot
and gherkins with the capers and
salt and pepper to taste. Pile in a
salad bowl. Pour over the
mayonnaise or French dressing and
garnish with the olives, lettuce
leaves, salami sausage and lemon
slices.

SERVES 6

MIXED SUMMER VEGETABLE SALAD

3 large new potatoes
3 new turnips
200 g/7 oz shelled peas
a small bunch of new carrots
French dressing
15 ml/1 tbsp chopped parsley
5 ml/1 tsp chopped fresh mint

Cook the vegetables and slice the carrots, potatoes and turnips. Reserve some of each vegetable for garnish and toss the rest in the French dressing with the herbs. Put the mixture in a serving dish and garnish with the reserved vegetables. Baste with a little more dressing.

SERVES 4 TO 6

MIXED WINTER VEGETABLE SALAD

1 cauliflower
2 large carrots
1 parsnip or 2 turnips
1 cooked beetroot
1 (225 g/8 oz) can peas
French dressing
watercress or fine cress

Steam the cauliflower, carrots, and parsnip or turnips. Divide the cauliflower into sprigs. Dice the carrots, parsnip or turnip, and beetroot, or cut into neat rounds with a cutter. Rinse and drain the peas.

Mix all the trimmings and uneven pieces of vegetable lightly with French dressing – include some of the peas. Put this mixture into a dish, preferably oblong. Cover with lines of each vegetable, very neatly arranged and with suitable colours adjoining. Garnish the edges with watercress or fine cress. Baste the surface with French dressing.

SERVES 6

MAYONNAISE

2 egg yolks (at room temperature)
salt and pepper
mustard powder
150–300 ml/¼–½ pint best olive oil
(at room temperature)
mixed vinegars to taste – 4 parts wine
vinegar or lemon juice, 2 parts
tarragon and 1 part chilli vinegar

Remove every trace of egg white from the yolks. Put the yolks in a thick basin which will stand steady in spite of vigorous beating. Add the salt, pepper and mustard to taste. Drop by drop, add the olive oil, beating or whisking vigorously all the time. As the mayonnaise thickens, the olive oil can be poured in a thin, steady stream but whisking must never slacken. When the mixture is really thick a few drops of vinegar or lemon juice stirred in will thin it again. Continue whisking in the oil, alternately with a little vinegar.

If the mayonnaise should curdle, break a fresh egg yolk into a clean basin and beat into this the curdled mixture drop by drop.

MAKES ABOUT 350 ml/12 fl oz

FRENCH DRESSING

30–45 ml/2–3 tbsp olive oil
salt and pepper
15 ml/1 tbsp wine vinegar or lemon
juice

Mix the oil and seasoning. Add the vinegar or lemon juice gradually, stirring constantly with a wooden spoon so that an emulsion is formed.

MAKES ABOUT 45 ml/3 tbsp

SOURED CREAM DRESSING

Stir some soured cream until smooth. Flavour with salt, pepper, prepared mustard and caster sugar. Add a little milk or top of the milk if too thick.

$\mathcal{S}$ANDWICHES

The sandwich was invented by the Earl of Sandwich in 1764, and modern versions of his snack (a slice of beef between two slices of bread) are still perfect as part of a light meal.

OPEN SANDWICHES

The appeal of these sandwiches lies in the artistic way in which the garnish is arranged. They must look colourful, fresh and tempting. Remember that garnishes stay fresher if arranged vertically and if kept under damp paper or cloth until serving time.

Use 5 mm/¼ inch thick slices of white or brown bread. Spread with softened butter and cover with different savoury mixtures. Garnish with stuffed olives, watercress sprigs or piped cream cheese.

Scrambled egg and crisply fried bacon, with cucumber and a twist of tomato.

Salami (without garlic) with raw onion rings and chopped parsley.

Liver pâté with mushrooms sautéed in butter, shreds of crisply fried bacon, small pieces of tomato, lettuce and gherkin.

Danish blue cheese with chopped apple coated with French dressing, topped with a parsley sprig.

Peeled prawns mixed with mayonnaise, topped with cucumber.

Hard-boiled egg slices sprinkled with cod's roe.

DOUBLE-DECKER SANDWICHES

Three thin slices of either brown or white bread are needed for each sandwich. Butter the slices thickly – the middle slice should be buttered on both sides – spread with two complementary fillings and sandwich together. Press together firmly so that the layers stick to each other.

Suggested fillings

1st layer – a slice of Cheddar cheese spread with mango chutney.
2nd layer – a mixture of grated raw apple and mayonnaise.

1st layer – slices of cold roast beef, spread with horseradish sauce.
2nd layer – watercress with thin slices of drained, pickled beetroot.

1st layer – cooked skinless pork sausage split lengthways.
2nd layer – grilled mushrooms.

TOASTED SANDWICHES

These make excellent dishes for late-night suppers, and are economical to produce since leftovers can often be used.

Toast the bread slices by grilling on one side only. Spread a suitable filling such as grated cheese mixed with apple slices and peanut butter all over the untoasted side. Grill the filling until crisp or bubbling. Top with a piece of bread toasted on both sides and garnish as wished.

Alternatively, toast the bread on both sides, butter one side of each slice and fill with a hot or cold, separately prepared filling, such as diced turkey and mushrooms in a cream sauce, or tuna and tomatoes moistened with a little mayonnaise.

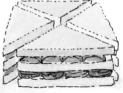

$\mathcal{P}$UDDINGS

Fresh fruit is often served after the main course of a supper, but sometimes it is a good idea to offer something a little more substantial such as an apple flan or a fruit fool.

FRUIT FOOL

about 675 g/1½ lb prepared fruit
caster sugar
*600 ml/1 pint pouring custard **or***
*double cream **or** 300 ml/½ pint*
custard and 300 ml/½ pint cream
mixed
lemon juice (optional)
ratafia biscuits

Cook the fruit if necessary. Strawberries, raspberries and loganberries should be crushed, sprinkled with caster sugar and left overnight.

Rub the fruit through a fine nylon sieve or purée in a blender. When cool, blend with the cold custard or cream; taste and sharpen with a little lemon juice if necessary. Sweeten to taste with caster sugar. Chill and serve with ratafia biscuits arranged carefully on top.

SERVES 6

RASPBERRY AND YOGURT DELIGHT

*1 (397 g/14 oz) can raspberries **or**
strawberries in syrup
15 ml/1 tbsp gelatine
300 ml/½ pint plain yogurt*

Drain the syrup from the fruit into a measuring jug and make it up to 250 ml/8 fl oz with water. Put 60 ml/4 tbsp of the measured syrup mixture into a small heatproof bowl and sprinkle the gelatine on to the liquid. Stand the bowl over a saucepan of hot water and stir until it has dissolved completely. Add the rest of the syrup.

Whisk the yogurt in a bowl until the curd is broken down evenly, and gradually whisk in the syrup mixture. Put in a cool place.

When the mixture is on the point of setting, fold in the drained fruit. Spoon into a serving dish and serve cool but not chilled.

SERVES 4

MANGO MOUSSE

1 kg/2¼ lb ripe mangoes
90 ml/6 tbsp fresh lime juice
100 g/4 oz caster sugar
15 ml/1 tbsp gelatine
2 egg whites
a pinch of salt
100 ml/3½ fl oz double cream
15 ml/1 tbsp light rum

Peel the fruit and cut the flesh off the stones. Purée with the lime juice in a blender or food processor. When smooth, blend in the sugar, then scrape the mixture into a bowl with a rubber spatula.

Place 45 ml/3 tbsp water in a small heatproof bowl. Sprinkle the gelatine on to the liquid. Stand the bowl over a saucepan of hot water and stir the gelatine until it has dissolved completely. Cool slightly, then stir into the mango purée.

In a clean, grease-free bowl, whisk the egg whites with the salt until they form fairly stiff peaks. Stir 15 ml/1 tbsp of the egg whites into the purée to lighten it, then fold in the rest.

Lightly whip the cream and rum together in a separate bowl, then fold into the mango mixture as lightly as possible. Spoon into a serving bowl. Refrigerate for about 3 hours until set.

SERVES 6 TO 8

FRESH FRUIT SALAD

*600 ml/1 pint water **or** fruit juice*
75 g/3 oz caster sugar
selection of prepared fruit
juice of 1 lemon
15 ml/1 tbsp brandy (optional)

Boil the water or fruit juice and sugar together until reduced to half quantity.

Pour sufficient syrup over the prepared fruit to cover it completely and flavour with lemon juice. Cover the bowl and allow the salad to become quite cold. Stir in the brandy, if used, a few minutes before serving. Serve with cream, custard, or ice cream.

MRS BEETON'S BAKEWELL PUDDING

*strawberry **or** apricot jam*
50 g/2 oz butter
50 g/2 oz caster sugar
1 egg
50 g/2 oz ground almonds
50 g/2 oz fine cake crumbs
a few drops of almond essence
icing sugar for dusting

SHORT CRUST PASTRY
100 g/4 oz plain flour
1.25 ml/¼ tsp salt
*50 g/2 oz margarine (**or** half butter, half lard)*
flour for rolling out

Set the oven at 200°C/400°F/gas 6. To make the pastry, sift the flour and salt into a bowl, then rub in the margarine until the mixture resembles fine breadcrumbs. Add enough cold water to make a stiff dough. Press the dough together lightly.

Roll out the pastry on a lightly floured surface and use to line an 18 cm/7 inch flan tin or ring placed on a baking sheet. Spread a good layer of jam over the pastry base.

In a mixing bowl, cream the butter with the sugar until pale and fluffy. Beat in the egg, then add the almonds, cake crumbs and essence. Beat until well mixed. Pour into the flan case, on top of the jam.

Bake for 30 minutes or until the centre of the pudding is firm. Sprinkle with icing sugar and serve hot or cold.

SERVES 4 TO 6

COEUR A LA CREME AU CITRON

150 ml/5 fl oz double cream
a pinch of salt
150 g/5 oz low-fat curd cheese
50 g/2 oz caster sugar
grated rind and juice of 1 lemon
2 egg whites

Line a 400 ml/14 fl oz heart-shaped coeur à la crème mould with greaseproof paper.

In a bowl whip the cream with the salt until it holds soft peaks. Break up the curd cheese with a fork, and whisk it gradually into the cream with the sugar. Do not let the mixture lose stiffness. Fold the lemon rind and juice into the cream as lightly as possible.

In a clean, grease-free bowl, whisk the egg whites until they hold stiff peaks. Fold them into the mixture, then very gently turn the mixture into the mould, filling all the corners.

Stand the mould in a large dish or roasting tin to catch the liquid which seeps from the mixture. Chill for at least 2 hours or overnight. Turn out and serve with single cream.

SERVES 6

SWEET OMELETTE

2 eggs
a pinch of salt
15 ml/1 tbsp single cream
15 g/½ oz caster sugar
15 g/½ oz unsalted butter
caster sugar for dredging

Beat the eggs thoroughly with the salt, cream and caster sugar. Heat the butter in an omelette pan and remove any scum. When the butter is really hot, pour in the egg mixture and stir until it begins to set. Fold away from the handle of the pan. Cook for another minute and then tip out on to a hot dish.

Dredge with caster sugar and serve at once.

Note Any sweet filling can be added, such as warmed jam, fruit purée or diced soft fruit. It should be spread evenly in the centre just before the omelette is folded over.

SERVES 2

THE PERFECT
OMELETTE

Mrs Beeton instructed cooks making an omelette to be 'particularly careful that it is not too thin, and, to avoid this, do not make it in too large a pan'. So, choose the right size pan – a two-egg omelette needs a 15 cm/ 6 inch pan.

*** Beat the eggs very thoroughly to incorporate plenty of air.

*** Melt a little butter in a hot pan, remove any scum and pour in the beaten eggs.

*** Reduce the heat, stir the eggs very gently until they begin to set. Cook until the top is just firm, then fold the edges over to form an oval shape and serve immediately.

*** Never make an omelette until just before it is to be eaten.

MRS BEETON'S APPLE FLAN

6 eating apples
4 cloves
45 ml/3 tbsp medium-dry sherry
30 ml/2 tbsp soft light brown sugar
3 egg whites
45 ml/3 tbsp caster sugar

SHORT CRUST PASTRY
175 g/6 oz plain flour
2.5 ml/½ tsp salt
75 g/3 oz margarine (or half butter, half lard)
flour for rolling out

Peel and core the apples, cutting each into eight sections. Put in a heatproof bowl, add the cloves and sherry and cover closely. Place the bowl in a deep saucepan. Add boiling water to come halfway up the sides of the bowl and cook for 20 minutes until the apple sections are tender but still intact.

Set the oven at 200°C/400°F/gas 6. Sift the flour and salt into a bowl, then rub in the margarine. Add enough cold water to make a stiff dough.

Roll out the pastry on a lightly floured surface and use to line a

23 cm/9 inch flan tin. Line the pastry with greaseproof paper and fill with baking beans. Bake for 10 minutes. Remove the paper and beans; cook for 5 minutes. Set aside.

Lower the oven temperature to 140°C/275°F, gas 1. Arrange the apples in the flan. Sprinkle with 30 ml/2 tbsp of the cooking liquid and the brown sugar.

In a clean, grease-free bowl, whisk the egg whites until stiff. Whisk in 10 ml/2 tsp of the caster sugar and spread lightly over the apples. Sprinkle the remaining sugar over. Bake for 1 hour. Serve warm or cold.

SERVES 6

LATE NIGHT SUPPER

*ham and egg pie
served with cheese and chutneys*

*Italian salad
served with mayonnaise*

fruit fool
or
fresh fruit

$\mathscr{I}$NDEX